Original title:
The Window Garden

Copyright © 2025 Creative Arts Management OÜ
All rights reserved.

Author: Mariana Leclair
ISBN HARDBACK: 978-1-80581-836-6
ISBN PAPERBACK: 978-1-80581-363-7
ISBN EBOOK: 978-1-80581-836-6

Nature's Promenade Beyond the Frame

In pots they sway, those silly greens,
With dance moves mimicking magazine scenes.
A cactus wearing shades, so cool,
While daisies gossip like kids at school.

A tomato blushing, thinking it's sweet,
A carrot's wiggle, what a treat!
The herbs all tease, it's quite a sight,
Parsley tells jokes under the moonlight.

The lettuce spins like a disco star,
And peppers play cards, sipping on a jar.
With ladybugs prancing, and ants on parade,
Every twitch and squirm, a grand charade.

Oh, what a sight from my little nook,
Nature throws parties; who needs a book?
So I sit and laugh at the playful show,
In my bright little patch, where funny things grow.

Sunbeams and Petal Dreams

Sunbeams dance on leaves so bright,
While flowers giggle in delight.
Bees are buzzing all around,
Dancing clumsily on the ground.

Pots with secrets line the sill,
Talking plants with sass and thrill.
In every pot, a tale unfolds,
Of wild adventures and marigold.

Hush of Flora in the City

In concrete jungles, blooms arise,
Chasing pigeons, oh what a surprise!
Lettuce debates with a tall fern,
While daisies gossip, waiting their turn.

A cactus in a party hat,
Wonders why it's not so fat.
It guards the door and greets the rain,
With prickly hugs, it entertains the lane.

Growth Beyond the Glass

Plants peep out, curious eyes,
Watching the world with a big surprise.
A tiny sprout in a tiny pot,
Dreams of a life where it's not forgot.

Sunflowers snooze, while mint makes tea,
Sharing secrets, just you and me.
The fern shakes hands with a quirky soil,
Laughing loud, their friendship a toil.

A Garden of Whispers

In a nook where whispers peek,
Petals laugh and softly speak.
A lazy tulip naps in the sun,
Claiming the edge, it's having such fun.

Basil teases, "I smell divine!"
But rosemary claims, "The kitchen's mine!"
They all unite with cheerful grins,
Celebrating life as the mischief begins.

A Symphony of Greens

In pots and trays, they wiggle and dance,
The herbs in rows take a silly stance.
Basil whispers jokes to a chatty thyme,
While lettuce laughs in the sun, feeling fine.

Peppers giggle, cloaked in bright attire,
While cucumbers plot to start a choir.
They sing of rain and frolic in breeze,
As carrots join in, with much ruckus and tease.

Sunflower Hues at Twilight

Sunflowers sway like they're on a stage,
With petals bright, they're the stars of the age.
They chat at dusk, gossiping like crows,
About who wore what, and where the wind blows.

Daisies giggle, comparing their height,
While pansies wonder if they'll get it right.
They burst into laughter, a colorful crew,
Painting the evening with a golden hue.

Nature's Embrace in Frames

In framed delights, the greens play peek-a-boo,
Potting soil jokes with the watering can, too.
The geraniums blush at the visitor's stare,
While ivy teases, hanging down without care.

Ferns are the dancers, twirling so spry,
As the air fills with scents that make us all sigh.
Each leaf and stem tells a wild little tale,
As the sun sets low, they begin to regale.

Scenic Serenity

Amidst the pots, a butterfly land,
With a flirt and a flutter, it gives us a hand.
The daisies are dreaming of trips to the beach,
While the mint chimes in, in a voice soft and breech.

With snickering roots and playful vines,
They plot a party, with sunshine and wines.
Let's toast the oddities in this little show,
Where laughter grows bright in a kinship we sow.

Echoes of Nature at Dusk

At twilight's hue, the plants all grin,
Crickets start their nightly spin.
A sneaky snail wears a tiny hat,
Chasing shadows—imagine that!

Squirrels dance, a wobbly show,
Twirling leaves and seeds they throw.
The moonlight giggles through the haze,
As flowers chatter in a maze.

Buzzing bees with comic flair,
They zip around without a care.
A cabbage rolls, claiming the stage,
In nature's playbook, it turns the page!

So raise a toast to blooms and bugs,
In this verdant land of joyful hugs.
With laughter seeping through the green,
Life's joke is sweet, and all unseen!

Reflections of Green in Steel and Stone

In city cracks, a petunia peaks,
Riding high on asphalt's streaks.
A dandelion with daring glee,
Winks at cars, oh look at me!

Through iron fences, ivy climbs,
Singing silly nursery rhymes.
A traffic cone dons leafy hats,
As gardeners whisper 'Hey, look at that!'

The squirrels conspire with the clock,
As pigeons watch—let's take stock!
They've plotted schemes for stolen fries,
In this green kingdom, such clever spies!

Who knew that nature, bold and bright,
Could thrive in concrete's tough plight?
With laughter woven in each vine,
The city bursts with life divine.

Reflections of Greenery

A pot of gold, or so they say,
Is just a cactus, on display.
It jabs your dreams with spiny facts,
While flowers giggle at their acts!

Basil whispers secrets to thyme,
'We're the herbs that break the crime!'
While lettuce stretches, green and bright,
'Take my leaf, it feels just right!'

A pumpkin dreams of Halloween,
While others plot a salad scene.
Each leaf a joker, happy and spry,
Crafting mischief as they lie!

So let this garden be your cheer,
With herbs and beans to spread the cheer.
The humor blooms in every part,
A verdant smile in every heart.

Whispers of Petals

Petals lean in, they share a laugh,
As grasses tease the garden staff.
'You're all so tall, we quite adore,
But watch your heads, or you'll hit the floor!'

A bee in shades sips nectar sweet,
While daisies dance to the happy beat.
A flower pranks, and oh what fun,
It hides from sun until it's done!

Butterflies flare in vivid hues,
They flutter by, winking to snooze.
'You think you can catch me?' they prance,
While bees look on, ready to dance!

So here's to life, both wild and free,
In this yard of whimsy, come see!
Every petal spins a tale,
With laughter echoing in the gale!

Tapestry of Growth

In pots so small, a riot blooms,
Tiny veggies chase away their glooms.
A carrot whispers, 'I'm not a stick!'
While lettuce giggles, 'That's quite a trick!'

Each sprout plays tag in the sunlight's ray,
Bouncing around in a leafy ballet.
'Look at me grow!' shouts a bold little pea,
Dancing with joy, as proud as can be.

Snapshots of Serenity

Succulents smile in their fancy dress,
Cacti poke fun, but don't mean to stress.
'Needles for the boys,' the daisies chime,
While ferns just wave, 'We're so out of time!'

A pot of mint laughs, 'I smell great tonight!'
Parsley dreams of a dance in the light.
Basil tells tales of a pesto so grand,
While thyme, always late, just can't understand.

Botanical Kaleidoscope

Petunias prance in a rainbow parade,
While mushrooms giggle, 'We're not afraid!'
'Watch us twirl,' cries a round pumpkin's hat,
As marigolds cheer, 'Hey, imagine that!'

Herbs chat about who's most herb-alicious,
Basil winks, 'I can be quite vicious!'
A sunflower leans, trying to impress,
While daisies in laughter wear floral dress.

Nature's Whispering Veil

In the morning light, the cosmos joins in,
Flowers gossip, 'Is it time for a spin?'
Bee balm beckons with a sweet little tune,
Hummingbirds laugh, 'Forget the balloon!'

A sunflower boasts, 'I'm the tallest of all!'
While roses roll eyes, 'You're just a tall ball!'
With each blooming bud, the laughter takes flight,
In this little patch, everything's light!'

Glass Fragments of Nature

Tiny seeds in pots, they grow,
Peeking out with a cheeky glow.
Chasing sunlight, they do prance,
In their merry, leafy dance.

Ladybugs, with spotted flair,
Dancing round without a care.
While snails slide by, a slow parade,
In this quirky, green charade.

Oh, the leaves do giggle bright,
Tickled by the moon's soft light.
Pollen jokes, they surely play,
In this lively, green ballet.

As raindrops tap on glass so sweet,
Plants tap-dance to the beat.
In a world so small and grand,
With nature's joy, we take a stand.

Urban Blooms in Light

Petunias peep through bricks and grime,
Chasing sunlight, having a prime.
Cacti in a narrow vase,
Sporting smiles, a prickly grace.

Bees in bow ties zoom and zoom,
Buzzing 'round in their bright room.
Sunflowers stand as high as dreams,
Tickling clouds with their silly beams.

Windowsills, a secret stage,
Where greens perform, free from cage.
With every leaf, a giggle flies,
As laughter dances near the skies.

Birds snicker at the urban scene,
Living life in a leafy green.
While kitchens smell of pumpkin pie,
Plants wink at clouds drifting by.

Serenity Beyond Panes

Behind the glass, a leafy crop,
Potatoes think they're a flower shop.
Radishes grinning, drawing your eye,
In a world where veggies fly high.

Herbs whisper secrets of delight,
While chives chuckle in the moonlight.
Basil daydreams of pasta fame,
Mint claims it's all just a game.

Through the glass, a cat does pounce,
On imaginary mice, it bounces.
While peppers blush with a rosy hue,
In a garden so lively, it's true.

Sunset spills its color spree,
As colors dance like a jubilee.
Laughing leaves in a gentle breeze,
Crafting stories with such ease.

Hidden Flora in Steel Frames

In city's grip, green tales unfold,
Silly flowers, brave and bold.
Hiding 'neath the watchful steel,
Their cheeky charm, a daily meal.

Fern fronds twirl, a waltz so fine,
On rooftop gardens, they do dine.
With sun hats made of cloud and light,
They giggle through the day and night.

Potted pals on every ledge,
Brightly cheer in a leafy pledge.
In the concrete jungle's heart,
Flora plays its funny part.

Sprouts poke heads in joyous cheer,
Whispering jokes for all to hear.
In funky pots, they wiggle free,
Crafting laughter in harmony.

Framing the Wild

In pots they plot their leafy dreams,
A fern conspires with the sunbeams.
The cactus teases, 'Touch me not!'
While rosemary's in a fragrant spot.

Around the sill, they dance and sway,
A quirky ballet, come what may.
The herbs all giggle, don't be shy,
As dirt flies up, oh my, oh my!

Fragrant Corners of Light

Basil whispers sweet, 'Have a taste!'
While mint declares, 'Oh, what a waste!'
The thyme rolls eyes, with zest so spry,
'Let's spice it up', it hums on high.

Petunias argue, red or blue?
The violets think the world's askew.
Together they laugh, they bicker and blend,
A fragrant joys that never end!

Botanical Stories Behind Glass

Behind each pane, a tale unfolds,
With daisies gossiping, being bold.
The succulents dream of a wild spree,
As parsley claims, 'I've got the key!'

A spider's web, a leafy lace,
While popcorn plants start a silly race.
The violets cheer, 'Hooray for me!'
In sunlit realms, they feel so free.

Nature's Tender Touch

The daisies tickle the morning light,
While dandelions plan a silly flight.
With laughter shared in every bloom,
They conjure joy to fill the room.

The orchids tease with colors bright,
As sundews catch the day so light.
In comical glee, they wiggle and dance,
In this green world, they take their chance.

Green Dreams in Brick and Mortar

In pots so round, my dreams take flight,
The cat thinks they're a cozy sight.
With every sprout, a leafy head,
They dance and twirl, when I'm in bed.

A bean will climb and wave hello,
While peas play peek just like a show.
I'll sprinkle love, and watch them grow,
Together we'll steal the garden show.

Who needs the sun, when there's a glow,
From a moth that thinks it's a disco?
Each sticky leaf just wants to spin,
In this wild world, we'll always win!

The radish grins, the carrots cheer,
A funny troupe that's always near.
In the cracks of bricks, they like to play,
In laughs and green, we'll spend the day.

The Hidden Chorus of Flora

In quiet corners, laughter blooms,
With giggles hiding in the fumes.
The daisies wink, the ferns all sway,
They plot their fun in foliage play.

A tulip tells the tale of bees,
While dandelions tease the breeze.
The violets burst in purple hues,
In concert grand, they share the news.

A spinach leaf dons its best attire,
And shimmies forth, igniting fire.
In leafy laughter, they unite,
With whispers soft, they take to flight.

The pots are filled with giggling greens,
A plant parade of lively scenes.
In sunlight's glow, they strut and pose,
The funniest sight that nature knows.

Glistening Dew on Leafy Abodes

In early morn, the dew drips bright,
Like pearls that tease the sun's first light.
The leaves stand proud, all dressed in cheer,
A morning party starts right here.

A raindrop slips, a squirrel takes stock,
As daisies laugh around the block.
With every glint, they giggle sweet,
Nature's humor can't be beat.

The herbs will chat, with minty breath,
While chives roll dice, defying death.
Each bead of dew, a tiny joke,
In this green world, fun's never broke.

The sun will rise, the shadows creep,
But in this garden, joy's a leap.
So come and play in leafy lanes,
Where laughter grows, and nothing wanes.

Nature's Embrace Through Stained Glass

Through colored panes, the sun will tease,
While plants below sway with the breeze.
They giggle softly, dressed in hue,
A rainbow of silliness to pursue.

The flowers peek in shades so bright,
They plot their fun from morn to night.
Each shadow tells a tale so grand,
In this embrace, we'll make our stand.

The vines will twist and climb with glee,
As petals wink, 'Come laugh with me!'
In every flicker, life unfolds,
With secrets bold, and dreams untold.

So here we sit, in joy's own space,
With nature's charms—a warm embrace.
Our leafy friends, they bloom and sway,
In stained glass light, we find our play.

Blossoming Perspectives

In pots of dreams, plants dance and sway,
They gossip about squirrels with much to say.
Sunshine spills jokes, petals start to grin,
With every new bloom, the laughter begins.

Watering cans chuckle, and soil gets wise,
As daisies tease tulips with colorful lies.
Bees don their hats, buzzing like pros,
In this garden theatre, the fun never slows.

Nature's Visions on Display

Roses wear spectacles, peeking around,
While daisies discuss who's the most profound.
A snail in a shell, a slow-moving sage,
Recites every tale like a wise, wrinkled page.

A frog on a leaf croaks an old tune,
His voice quite the crooner beneath the bright moon.
Mockingbird mischief, oh what a prank,
As they steal all the worms from the neighbor's bank.

Kaleidoscope of Leaves

Leaves twirl and tumble, they dance and they play,
In hues like a rainbow, they set the day.
A squirrel in striped socks shows off his flair,
While caterpillars argue about who can share.

Sunbeams tickle roots, oh what a sight,
Digging up laughter, from morning till night.
The tomatoes are winking, the peppers become,
A band of green veggies, all ready to hum.

Secrets Held in Light

In a patch of sunshine, mischief unfolds,
With shadows of critters, their stories retold.
A ladybug giggles, wearing red spots,
As the ants march in lines, plotting their plots.

Butterflies flutter in capes made of bliss,
Whispering secrets, you wouldn't want to miss.
A garden of wonder, where laughter takes flight,
In a world full of whimsy, all wrapped up tight.

Garden of Reflections

In a pot, a cactus grins,
Its prickles laugh, their humor spins.
A daisy dons a silly hat,
While chatting with a friendly rat.

The herbs are planning a grand show,
Mint brings salsa, oh what a flow!
Thyme's got jokes that just won't quit,
And basil's dance makes everyone split.

Petunias wear their brightest hues,
Flaunting outfits like morning blues.
Violets giggle, blushing deep,
In this patch, secrets run and leap.

With every leaf, a whispered jest,
In our patch, we're truly blessed.
That garden's not just roots and dirt,
It's full of joy, no space for hurt.

The Hush of Plant Life

In the corner, ferns like to sway,
All the while, they really play.
With gossip on the breeze, they share,
While pretending they don't even care.

Pansies plotting mischief bright,
They snicker softly, out of sight.
A mint leaf sneezes, oh what a fuss,
And worms roll over, just to discuss.

The pots are filled with tales untold,
Each sprout's a story, brave and bold.
When sunbeams peek in, they all conspire,
To weave their yarns higher and higher.

Laughter sprinkles from leaf to stem,
In quiet roots, they jest like them.
In this hush, life's odd little quirks,
Bring smiles forth in all their works.

Fleeting Flora Fables

Once a tulip dreamed to fly,
With petals wide beneath the sky.
It jumped up high, and what a flop,
Now it tells tales from the crop.

A flower pot thought it could dance,
With twirling blooms, it took a chance.
But with one spin, it wobbled hard,
And rolled away, quite unbarred.

Chives wear scarves, looking so neat,
Chanting verses, oh what a feat!
While daisies pretend to read the news,
Laughing at stories in mismatched shoes.

In this garden, fables bloom bold,
Each petal whispers secrets untold.
With humor sprouting where thoughts collide,
In capers and giggles, they take pride.

Serenity in Sunlight

Sunlight peeks at leafy greens,
Where every plant has silly dreams.
A radish hides, its blushy face,
Hopes to win the 'Most Shy' race.

The sunflower strikes a goofy pose,
With neighbor daisies forming rows.
A gentle breeze begins to tease,
While ants march past, ignoring ease.

Tomatoes giggle, round and red,
Beneath the sun, they jump from bed.
The melons roll in playful glee,
Inviting all for a fruity spree.

With every sway, the laughter flows,
In this bright patch, humor grows.
Serenity found in cheerful sprout,
Makes all who visit smile about.

Fragrant Blossoms at Dawn

In pots they sit, so snug and tight,
With happy greens, they greet the light.
One rose complained it felt too small,
"Can't we stretch and have a ball?"

The daisies laughed, they wore a crown,
"We'll dance around, please don't frown!"
Then came a bee, all buzz and cheer,
"Who invited me? I smell a beer!"

Chives played hide and seek with thyme,
As morning sun began its climb.
"Oh look! A squirrel!" cried one sweet bud,
"Hey buddy, toss us down some mud!"

With every leaf and tiny sprout,
Their antics left no room for doubt.
Laughter echoed through the air,
In this little green, happy square.

Whispering Leaves in Light

Leaves gossip gently, in the breeze,
"Did you see that? A slip of cheese!"
A ladybug with great delight,
Said, "I found a crumb, oh what a sight!"

Sunlight flickers, shadows play,
"I'm the leaf that won't decay!"
Said one who flaunted every spot,
"While you all wilt, I'm boiling hot!"

The pansies chuckled, pink and bright,
"We'll throw a party, what a sight!"
With petals open wide and gay,
"Bring your snacks, we'll dance all day!"

Dandelions join in on the fun,
"Make a wish, you're number one!"
In this watercolor parade,
Beneath the sun, all doubts now fade.

Reflections on Glass

On the sill, a leafy crew,
Each one claims a special view.
"I see a cat, it's napping there!"
"Not fair! It doesn't have to share!"

The sunbeam slips, a golden thief,
"Hey, shine on me!" cried one green leaf.
While violets claimed the choicest spot,
"Don't block my shine! You've missed the lot!"

The ferns exchanged their whispered dreams,
"I long to float on gentle streams!"
But then they sighed, with hopes set low,
"Will we ever get to go?"

Nearby, a bird took quite a stare,
"What's the fuss? Do I smell flair?"
And with a chirp, he flew away,
While plants just laughed, "We're here to stay!"

Petals in the Breeze

Petals float like pink balloons,
Dancing lightly, making tunes.
"Catch me quick!" a tulip cried,
"But don't let me tumble, I'll slide!"

A sunflower yawned, stretched out wide,
"I'll join your game! Let's go outside!"
The wind agreed, with gentle hands,
"Let's twirl and twist across the lands!"

"Oh dear, a bird!" yelled out a rose,
"Will she eat us? Who really knows?"
But then it laughed, just flew on by,
"What a day! Just look at us fly!"

Longing for fun, the blossoms gleamed,
"Let's play tag until we've dreamed!"
As petals swayed, the laughter teased,
In nature's dance, they all were pleased.

Life Beyond the Sill

In pots of dreams, my plants do dance,
With leaves that frolic and prance.
They miss the sun, but love the rain,
While plotting schemes to drive me insane.

The basil sings and thyme does cheer,
While I just wish they'd disappear.
They gossip loud about the flies,
While I grow weary of their lies.

A cactus laughs, a fern just sighs,
Their antics bright as summer skies.
Each day I water, pray and fret,
But soon this foliage will be my pet.

I'll try to teach them etiquette,
Who knew that plants could be so pet?
With every sprout, a new delight,
My silly garden, pure and bright.

Colors of Contemplation

Behold the hues, a vibrant mess,
Each petal dressed in fancy dress.
The daisies wink, the violets grin,
While I wonder what lies within.

Marigolds gossip about the sun,
While orchids try to out-fun.
With bees that buzz in jest, you see,
This lively crew is quite the spree!

The tulips take turns striking poses,
While my drooping ferns look like roses.
I ponder if they plan a show,
Where weeds might dance and wildflowers grow.

Each color calls, a playful spark,
A rainbow smiles when day turns dark.
In this odd place, joy's always near,
Living art, my world sincere.

Enchanted Panes

Behind the glass, mischief brews,
Where pots conspire, and sunlight shoes.
A tiny gnome inflicts his charm,
While pepper plants plot and swarm.

The shadows play hide and seek,
A mischievous game, oh so unique.
I've lost count of the whispers heard,
From leafy conspirators, in each word.

A minty breeze with secrets flies,
While clouded dramas spill the lies.
They spin tall tales of summer's grace,
While I just laugh at their funny face.

Each pane reflects a curious sight,
Where laughter blooms in morning light.
Through glassy walls, where shadows play,
The garden's whims will always stay.

Cultivating Calm

A pot of peace sits on the shelf,
With plants that giggle at the self.
The soil's rich with laughter's mirth,
And every leaf knows its own worth.

The chives debate on what's for lunch,
While mint declares, it's time to munch!
With every water drop I pour,
These green delights just want to roar.

A stone sits quietly, full of grit,
While potted pals find the perfect hit.
They dance around this tranquil space,
In their green world, it's a merry place.

With each new sprout, my worries fade,
In this odd realm, I've surely strayed.
My garden giggles, calm yet wild,
In this escape, I'm nature's child.

Nature's Canvas Unframed

A cactus posed with flair,
In bright green shoes, it's so debonair.
The daisy tried to dance with glee,
But tripped on roots while sipping tea.

The basil dreams of being a star,
While mint thinks it's a spicy bar.
The orchids giggle in their dress,
They hold their petals, more or less!

The sun peeks in to steal the show,
The gnome just blinks, he doesn't know.
With quirky plants, the laughter swells,
A wild, green party, who can't you tell?

In this chaos of leafy pranks,
Each flower gives their silly thanks.
With nature's brush, they paint their cheer,
A merry canvas, year after year.

Botanical Dreams Beyond Glass

Peeking outside, the fern had dreams,
Of racing squirrels and flowing streams.
The spider spun her web with glee,
While hummingbirds sang silly, carefree.

A rose declared her royal stance,
Swaying gently, longing for a chance.
The daisies joined in a funky jig,
Teasing the tulips, small and big.

The sunflowers cracked a big ol' smile,
Winking at passersby for a while.
With cheeky sprouts beneath the light,
Each step of whimsy feels so right!

Their laughs drift up, a joyous sound,
In this glassy world, fun is found.
A botanical bash, no need for air,
Dreams bloom wildly, with silly flair.

The Secret Oasis

In a plant pot, a party stirs,
With whispers of petals and lively furs.
The ivy plays peek-a-boo with time,
While careful sunbeams chime and rhyme.

A gnome with charm guards the door,
While creeping vines seek galore.
The violets gossip, oh so sly,
About the tulips with a winked eye.

Ferns like fans cheer for all,
As plump tomatoes prepare for a ball.
With playful pots and a quirky crew,
Every day brings something new.

In this bright, hidden, leafy dome,
Nature's lunacy feels like home.
So let your worries take a break,
Join the plants for a giggle to make!

Glistening Leaves at Dusk

At dusk, the leaves wear shiny coats,
As they gather 'round to swap their notes.
The oak shares tales of its old bark,
While nearby, a squirrel makes a snark.

"I'm king of nuts!" the acorn shouts,
While ferns roll eyes, planting doubts.
The mint jokes about a tea party,
With breezes blowing, oh so hearty!

A sunflower checks its golden crown,
As violets blush, feeling down.
The wisteria sings a lullaby sweet,
While critters stomp their tiny feet.

In this glimmering, whimsical space,
The laughter and sparkle fills the place.
With every leaf, a chuckle to lend,
In the quirkiest garden, on joy we depend!

Quietude Encased

Potted plants dressed in their best,
Always waiting for a guest.
They gossip softly, leaf to leaf,
Sharing secrets, oh what a belief!

Sunlight sneaks in through the glass,
To tickle each stem, and make them laugh.
With a twist and a turn, all sprout a grin,
Plant humor is best when it's grown within!

A cactus jokes, 'I'm prickly yet fun!'
While daisies dance, making a run.
Whispers of growth, oh what a show,
In this tiny realm, the laughter flows!

From watering cans to pots so round,
Laughter and soil mix, joy is found.
In silence they thrive, yet in glee they bask,
Such are the tales in their verdant flask!

Afternoon Sunlit Tales

As the clock strikes two in a sunny room,
Miracles happen, dispelling the gloom.
Every leaf wiggles, shakes off the dust,
As petals burst forth, it's truly a must!

A fern tells a joke, quite leafy and light,
Promises laughter by the end of the night.
The pothos chuckles, 'I'm hanging around!'
While a geranium snickers, 'Look at me, I'm crowned!'

With shadows dancing, the sun starts to tease,
Saying, "Let's play hide and seek, if you please."
Rhododendrons giggle, spinning with glee,
In this patch of joy, they're all wild and free!

Potting mix and petals, what a funny spree,
Nature's tableau, full of humor and glee.
In this sunlit show, we're all in good cheer,
With each little bloom, it all becomes clear!

Whispered Hues of Joy

In the still of the day, colors burst bright,
With laughter like petals, taking off in flight.
A tangerine bloom whispers a cheer,
To the lavender buds that chuckle near!

Tiny pots lined up, like a comedy crew,
With jokes taking root, oh what fun to brew!
The sunbeams wink as they spill through the panes,
Making every bloom dance with joy, no strains!

'You're looking stunning, dear fuchsia friend!'
Said the shy little violet with a twinkle to send.
In shades so merry, the colors inspire,
For whispered jokes light up like a fire!

What wonders grow when the sun starts to play,
With giggles of petals at the close of the day.
Life among green, such mischievous delight,
Every glance brings smiles, from morning to night!

Seasonal Secrets Unveiled

Spring bursts forth with a comedic flair,
With every bloom, there's a joke to share.
The daffodils burst, 'We are the sunny crew!'
While tulips shout, 'Hey, we're colorful too!'

Summer's warm touch gets the humor in bloom,
As sunflowers waltz, filling up every room.
'Life's a jest!' they declare with delight,
While sipping on sunlight from morning till night.

Autumn brings laughter, in hues of gold,
With leaves like confetti, stories unfold.
'We're all falling for you!' they chorus with glee,
As pumpkins roll in with a giggly decree!

Winter's frost paints a silvery scene,
Yet even in chill, the plants know what's keen.
Whispers of warmth pulse beneath icy skin,
In every season, the joy weaves within!

A Symphony of Bloom

Potted plants sway, dancing with glee,
As squirrels debate, 'Who will sip my tea?'
The tomatoes giggle, growing a ton,
While herbs throw a party, oh what fun!

The sun-drenched daisies wear hats so bright,
Chasing away shadows, a dazzling sight.
The carrots whisper jokes from below,
While onions just cry, they steal the show!

Bees hold a concert, buzzing so loud,
Petunias blush bright, feeling so proud.
Each leaf seems to twirl, a sight to see,
As nature's own dancers, wild and free.

With watering cans acting as drum,
The garden bursts forth with its own happy hum.
In this joyful patch, laughter ignites,
A symphony of blooms brings pure delights.

Secret Haven in the Sky

Up high in my fortress, so packed with plant,
Climbing vines plot mischief, they frolic and chant.
The spider spins webs, a cozy retreat,
While butterflies join as they dance to the beat.

Lettuce wears sunglasses, thinks it's so cool,
Bragging to radishes, 'I rule this pool!'
Chasing away gloom, they soak up the rays,
In this secret haven, humor always plays.

The clouds toss confetti, rain falls like cheers,
Tickling the daisies, banishing fears.
A squirrel's acorn-throwing, his aim isn't great,
Causes a chuckle, oh what a fate!

With laughter like sunshine brightening the air,
I share my adventures, no moment to spare.
In this high-flying patch, joy takes its aim,
A secret haven, where fun's not to blame.

The Light Beyond the Lattice

Through crisscrossed bars, light dances with cheer,
    Mischievous shadows hide, drawing near.
    Sunflowers gossip of bees that they know,
    While pepper plants plot to steal the show.

The chives tease the garlic, 'You stink up the place!'
    They laugh with the basil – oh what a race!
    Tomatoes and peppers hold a colorful ball,
    Where laughter erupts, and no one feels small.

A ladybug winks, suggests a wild game,
    While sprouts talk of futures, trying to frame.
    In the lattice light, there's magic to find,
    With fun little critters, happiness kind.

Beneath playful leaves, giggles do rhyme,
    In this quirky escape, every inch feels sublime.
    The light shines in brightly, a joyous parade,
    In this playful garden, jokes are well-made.

Seeds of Hope in Small Spaces

Little seeds chuckle, 'We might seem real small,
But wait 'til we grow, we'll have a great ball!'
Each tiny sprout thinks it's destined for fame,
In this crowded corner, they play their own game.

Ants march in line, a busy parade,
While snails hold a race, though slow, never fade.
The radish jokes loudly, 'I'm spicy, you see!'
While carrots grow tall, just dreaming to be.

In pots lined with laughter, herbs take their turn,
Sharing their scents, as the daylight does burn.
Each tiny bouquet shines brightly with cheer,
Seeds of hope giggle, spreading good cheer.

'To bloom and to play, is our garden's true aim,'
They shout as they flourish, unashamed, yet tame.
In these small spaces, joy truly blooms,
At the card table of life, where laughter consumes.

Shrubs and Serenity

In pots they sit, small and spry,
Whispering secrets to the sky.
With soil on leaves, they do conspire,
To grow their dreams, and never tire.

A squirrel once tried to take a peek,
But slipped and fell with quite the squeak.
The herbs just chuckled, light and free,
As if to say, 'Not meant for thee!'

The sunbeam tickles, a funny sight,
As petals sway in morning light.
They quirkily nod, a leafy jam,
Creating laughter, oh what a slam!

With every rain, a pitter-pat,
They giggle under, 'What's up with that?'
A garden full of jolly fuss,
Where plants decide to make a fuss.

The Dance of Leaves

In breezy waltz, the leaves do twirl,
With every gust, they spin and swirl.
A dance-off born from sunlight's kiss,
They laugh and shout, 'Oh, don't you miss?'

One leaf slips off, a tumbly show,
'Is it me, or did the wind just blow?'
With spins and flutters, they have a go,
'Then hold on tight, we're on a roll!'

The daisies chuckle, 'What a crew,
Who knew we'd get this silly too?'
As roots tap in a rhythm neat,
The whole green gang can't resist the beat!

And if you watch, you might just see,
The garden's antics are pure glee.
Through every twist, a smile's spread,
Fun among the plants instead!

Nature's Breath Against Glass

With morning dew upon the pane,
Nature giggles, bursting plain.
Waving grasses, soft and sly,
'Hello, viewer! Wanna try?'

A raindrop rolls, then goes kerplunk,
As clouds parade all big and junk.
The window shakes with every beat,
Like plants are bouncing to a tweet!

A bumblebee buzzes, a comedic show,
It mistook the glass for an open row.
"Oh dear, oh my, what's this I see?"
Then off it goes, quite humorously!

And as the sun begins to set,
A leafy laugh, we won't forget.
For nature's tricks, from here to there,
Remind us joy is everywhere.

Threads of Light and Leaf

In strands of sunlight, shadows play,
The leaves converge in a bright ballet.
With vines entwined, they share a tease,
'Come join our world; it's sure to please!'

A caterpillar, slow and proud,
Sheds off its skin, and feels so loud.
'Look at me! A fluffy ball!'
The flowers chuckle, 'Wanna crawl?'

Mossy blankets hug the ground,
Underneath, where fun is found.
And tiny snails, in their slow race,
Make every moment a funny chase.

At dusk the glowworms start to wink,
Crafting stories, they don't blink.
For every thread of light is sweet,
In nature's heart, forever neat.

Solace Amongst the Shadows

In pots of green, they dance with glee,
A cactus trying to be a tree.
The herbs are plotting their next big play,
As sneaky snails steal time away.

With laughter loud, the petals sway,
While sunbeams chase the clouds away.
A butterfly, in prankster mode,
Wears a face of mischief on his road.

Tiny ants march with flair and style,
Each thinking they're the garden's child.
In soil so rich, their dreams take flight,
While worms recite their poems at night.

Among the greens, the laughter flows,
In this haven where silliness grows.
With every sprout, a joke takes root,
In this humble, joyful little nook.

Views of Verdancy

Oh, what a sight, a leafy feast,
That broccoli thinks it's quite the beast.
Tomatoes blush, like shy young teens,
While carrots giggle behind the greens.

Up in the air, a flower sneezes,
A bee falls down, 'Oh, that's just breezy!'
Sunflowers stretch, with heads held high,
Saying, 'Look, I'm taller! No need to lie!'

In pots stacked high, there's chaos reign,
Bean vines tangled, oh what a pain!
Yet in this mess, joy finds a way,
As laughter blooms day after day.

With every sprig, a tale unfolds,
Of humor, joy, and dreams retold.
A garden game, a game of glee,
In leafy lanes, wild and free.

A Tapestry of Color

Whisking through blooms, a poet's delight,
Painted petals in morning light.
The daisies laugh, they wear their crowns,
While pansies make the silliest frowns.

The garden's a stage, a theater grand,
Where every flower has a band.
Roses in red, they sing out loud,
While violets whisper, 'Please, not so proud!'

In hues of humor, the daisies prance,
As bees all join in the dancing chance.
With pollen confetti, they spread the cheer,
In this botanical circus, the fun is near!

Colorful chaos, a vivid spree,
Where every shade brings more jubilee.
In this merry mix, we all will see,
Nature's joy in its wild spree.

The Quiet Murmur of Growth

In whispers soft, the seedlings sigh,
'Oh, how we love when clouds roll by!'
They giggle as raindrops start to play,
In nature's splash, they splash away.

The little sprouts whisper their dreams,
More than just veggies; they plot schemes.
A broccoli's dream of being a tree,
While radishes yearn for a life so free.

In twilight's glow, the shadows prank,
As moonlight dips into the bank.
With night's neat cloak, they share a joke,
From leafy lips, laughter awoke.

And in this hush, a humor blooms,
Mixing with scents from earthy rooms.
In every sprout, a chuckle swells,
In gardens where the laughter dwells.

Sunlit Sanctuaries

In a pot sat a chive, feeling so spry,
Said to a daisy, "Why not give it a try?"
"We could host a party, just us and a bee,"
Daisy chuckled back, "But I'm all out of tea!"

The sun beamed bright, casting shadows so wide,
A squirrel scampered by, looking for a ride.
"Hop on my leaves," the chive called with glee,
"We'll rule the garden! Just you wait and see!"

The birds chirped above, offering their tunes,
A crow joined the mix, cracking jokes like a goon.
"Why did the lettuce never win a race?"
"Because it always took time to pick up the pace!"

Laughter erupted from petals and stems,
In this tiny haven where nature's a gem.
They drank up the sunshine, with giggles and cheer,
In their sunlit sanctuary, nothing to fear!

Flora's Soliloquy

Petunia, quite proud, talked to her friend,
"I'm the belle of the ball, the style I transcend!"
A basil replied, rolling his green little eyes,
"You might have the blooms, but I've got the pies!"

"Oh please, dear basil, your food's all the rage,
But I'm here for glamour; I'm center stage!"
She swayed in the breeze, preparing her stance,
While the basil just chuckled, ready to prance.

Then came a zinnia, bold with her hue,
"Let's spice up this garden, we need something new!"
"I could pitch a show," the petunia proclaimed,
"All about glamour! I'd have it well-gamed!"

In the midst of their banter, a butterfly flew,
"What do you girls need? I could sprinkle some dew!"
"Stop by any time! Bring your friends for a dance,
In this floral fiesta, come join the romance!"

Frames of Tranquility

Behind the glass pane, secrets unfold,
With stories of sunflowers, daring and bold.
A cactus begins a tale of the west,
"I once stood my ground, I must say, I'm the best!"

A fern interjected, swaying with grace,
"Oh please, dear cactus, let's keep up the pace!"
"You've got your kin, but I've got my flair,
Bouncing with style, you should see my hair!"

Meanwhile, a geranium sighed with a wink,
"It's not about looks, it's all about the drink!"
"Bring out the nectar, a party we'll throw,
Imagine our fun, we'll steal the whole show!"

A neighbor named ivy chuckled in tune,
"I'd hang out with you guys, beneath the bright moon.
Let's fest until dawn, while the stars twinkle bright,
In this frame of tranquility, everything's right!"

Blossoms in Breezes

In the gentle wind, they danced and played,
A tulip exclaimed, "The sunshine's our aid!"
"Let's sway in a circle, show off our skills,
The bees will all come, let's give them some thrills!"

A violet chimed in, with a whiff of sass,
"I'm the queen of the garden, all the flowers in class!"
But roses rolled petals, oblivious to the game,
"With our smell so divine, we'll surely bring fame!"

Laughter erupted; even daisies would spin,
"Let's throw in some zests, let the fun now begin!"
The daisies started cracking jokes, oh so bold,
"Why do the flowers never get old?"

"Because they all bloom, but never grow cold!"
With giggles and winks, they blossomed their way,
In the breezy enchantment, they turned night to day!

Petals Whispering Dreamscapes

Petals dance with giggles bright,
Fluttering soft in morning light.
Bees play tag from flower to flower,
Stealing nectar, sweet as a shower.

Garden gnomes take a frolic spree,
Waving at the bumblebee.
Sunbeams slide, a playful chase,
As shadows wink, a joyful face.

Daisies wear their polka dots,
While ants debate on picnic plots.
Whimsical leaves twist and twine,
Sharing secrets in nature's shrine.

Laughter peeks from every inch,
As snails slide slow, not a pinch.
Whispered dreams in colors bold,
In this garden, joy unfolds.

Enclosed Nature's Heart

Within this box, wild things do grow,
Plants and critters put on a show.
A ladybug spins a tiny tale,
As worms giggle, soft and pale.

A cactus grins with prickly might,
While violets blush, delighting in sight.
Sunshine sprays a golden grin,
Against the wall, the fun begins.

Chirping birds wear hats of cheer,
While rabbits plot snacks, oh so near.
A playful breeze swirls around,
As daisies twirl and spin on ground.

Bubbles float in frothy air,
As mischief blooms everywhere.
A patch of green with laughter spun,
Nature's heart is never done.

Sill Stories

On my sill, a tale begins,
With tiny leaves, all winks and grins.
A sprout tells secrets, sweet and spry,
While chubby raindrops bounce by.

Herbs rehearse for the hungry crew,
Spices whisper what they can do.
Tomatoes giggle with a red-faced flair,
As mint teases with its cool air.

A squirrel swings from the flower pot,
Munching on seeds that he forgot.
Cacti chuckle at sunburned feet,
While the basil dreams of something sweet.

Frogs croak verses to the charming buzz,
In this tiny world that just because.
Sill stories spun in mirth and cheer,
Nature's laughter, loud and clear.

Heartbeats of Green

In the green, a funny beat,
Frogs and crickets find their feet.
Every bloom shakes with delight,
As nature dances, day and night.

A petunia spins, it's quite the sight,
While pickles in jars ooze out with fright.
Leaves play hide and seek with the sun,
Radiating joy, oh what fun!

Little bugs don their fancy shoes,
Chasing after the morning dew.
Sassy snails jot down their plans,
With tiny pens and tiny hands.

In this verdant, living scene,
Heartbeats echo, laughs serene.
Every corner hums a tune,
In the garden's afternoon.

Fragrant Echoes of Season

In a pot, a sprout stood tall,
Wondering why it couldn't crawl.
It watched the birds take to the air,
And thought, 'Why can't I go anywhere?'

Bees buzzed round with a silly hum,
While I held a leaf that looked like gum.
The gardener laughed and snipped a stem,
Saying, 'This mint tastes bad for men!'

Lush Vistas in Corners

In the corner, a plant takes a peek,
Sipping sunlight, feeling quite cheeky.
Next to it, a cactus wore a grin,
'Prickly pear, let the fun begin!'

A sunflower giggled at the shade,
'My friends, don't let your beauty fade!'
While a rogue fern tried to do a dance,
Stomping roots, it took a chance.

petals against the sky

Petals flapping like they're on a spree,
Saying, 'Catch me, I'm wild and free!'
A busy bee buzzed by in a suit,
Dropping pollen like confetti loot.

The sky winked down with a blue-tinted grin,
Saying, 'You silly blooms, let the fun begin!'
As the clouds chuckled at all the fuss,
A raindrop fell, 'Hey, you forgot us!'

Urban Eden in View

In a windowsill, the herbs are sly,
Hiding from pigeons that flutter by.
The basil whispers to the thyme,
'Let's make a sauce that's truly sublime!'

A cheeky radish popped up to say,
'I'm rootin' for you in every way!'
While the parsley shakes its leafy crown,
Saying, 'In this city, we won't frown!'

Confined Beauty

In a pot high above the street,
A cactus dreams of being neat.
It pokes a neighbor through the glass,
"Hey buddy, how's it feel to pass?"

The herbs gossip about the sun,
"Too close, too far, we're never done!"
They roll their leaves in pure dismay,
"Let's throw a party, hip hip hooray!"

The blooms have fun with all their hues,
Dancing in light, with sneaky views.
"A pigeon's come! Quick, strike a pose!"
"Is my makeup right? Do I have growth woes?"

But at night, they settle down to rest,
Counting stars—a leafy quest.
"Tomorrow's a chance for mischief anew,
Let's prank the humans, just me and you!"

Blooms in Urban Spaces

Rooftops packed with playful blooms,
Whisper stories of leafy rooms.
They laugh at traffic, honks, and fuss,
"Are we plants or a circus bus?"

Tiny tomatoes start a race,
"Who can grow the most in this space?"
A lettuce leaf rolls its eyes,
"I'm not here for any prize!"

Bumblebees buzzing, tickle my face,
"Dance with us in this tiny space!"
Sunflowers wear their hats with pride,
"See how I reach—I'm in the vibe!"

When clouds drift in, they throw a fit,
"Cover our rooftop, not a bit!"
Yet settle down when the rain pours,
"Now's a spa day, no chores, no doors!"

Dreaming in Colors

Each petal tells a vibrant tale,
In shades that never seem to pale.
"Look at me, I'm bright and bold!"
"Can you beat this? I'm pure gold!"

A daisy asked a rose one day,
"Why do the bees come out to play?"
The rose replied with a shrug,
"Maybe they like our lovely mug!"

Chives are whispering spicy dreams,
"Muffins made from us, it seems."
"You're just jealous of my flair,
I'm the garnish, fresh and rare!"

Together they laugh at the busy street,
"Who knew our lives would be so sweet?"
With each flower reaching higher,
They bloom in joy, never tire!

A Glimpse of Wilderness

In tiny pots, wild dreams take flight,
Legends of jungles come alive at night.
"Do you think we'll ever be free?"
"Only if the squirrels agree!"

A fern with curls tells secrets low,
"Every petal's got a show!"
"Let's break out, let's roam the park!"
"Only if it's not too dark!"

Vines climb up, making quite a mess,
"Oops, I knocked the coffee press!"
"Watch out for that jumping frog!"
"Or we'll be stuck in this wild hog!"

But when the moonlight starts to beam,
They dream of fields, their endless scheme.
"We'll grow wild, we'll set our pace,
For now, we'll dance in this small place!"

Shadows of Blossoms

In the sun, they play hide and seek,
Petals giggle, like kids at their peak.
Leaves whisper secrets to passing bees,
While squirrels practice acrobatic fees.

A flower sneezes, pollen goes airborne,
Bees wear tiny masks, looking all torn.
A plant in a pot wants to break out,
Dreaming of gardens, oh what a clout!

Inside, the herbs throw a tiny rave,
Dancing in dirt, not wishing to behave.
Basil pairs salsa with thyme's ballet,
What a wild party, hip-hip-hooray!

The cactus is stoic, the star of the show,
While succulents giggle at their own glow.
Their thorns are a joke, a prickly charade,
Yet no one minds, they love the parade!

Glimpse of Earth's Palette

Colors collide in sunlight's warm glow,
Crayons of flora, putting on a show.
Tomatoes are blushing, radishes laugh,
Painting the world, a green and red staff.

The sunflowers chuckle, so tall and bright,
While daisies debate if it's day or night.
A rainbow appears in the broccoli's crown,
Veggies in wigs, all ready to clown.

Petunia's periwinkle, so fine and rare,
Spills her shades with a flamboyant flare.
While herbs get all tangled like spaghetti strands,
Basil calls out, "I'm a part of the bands!"

In this riot of hues, joy is a must,
We dance with the dirt, we revel in rust.
Who knew that a patch could be so profound?
With giggles and greens, pure silly joy found!

Urban Wilderness Displayed

In concrete jungles, plants boldly sprout,
Claiming their space, shouting, "We're not out!"
Miniature forests on balconies wake,
Pigeons play tag while the sun's on break.

A fern waves hello to the passing cat,
While ivy invites birds to have a chat.
Cement doesn't stop the wild from its quest,
Neighbors peek out, they're underplant guests!

Windows are stages, a plant parade blooms,
With pots for costumes, not one set of brooms.
Succulents gossip about their green flair,
While herbs critique roses' perfume affair.

The pineapple's dreaming of tropical seas,
As kale and chard join in, singing with ease.
What a sight to see in this urban delight,
Nature's in charge, we're all invited tonight!

Roots Reaching for Light

Underneath, the roots are having a blast,
Stretching and creeping, they're growing so fast.
They whisper and giggle, the soil their stage,
Plotting their climb like a secret sage.

"Why's the grass greener?" a root does declare,
"Let's dig for answers! There's light in the air!"
Their little adventure, a game of delight,
Poking and prodding, reaching for light.

Cabbage and carrots all cheer from below,
A community effort, putting on a show.
Leeks play the piano with roots like fine strings,
As radishes hum in their earthy swing.

The quest for sunlight, a root's golden dream,
In a pot or a patch, they're part of the team.
In a funny ballet, they shimmy and sway,
Finding their way, come what may!

www.ingramcontent.com/pod-product-compliance
Lightning Source LLC
Chambersburg PA
CBHW070320120526
44590CB00017B/2753